Mexican
CUISINE

Enslow
PUBLISHING

BY SOPHIE
WASHBURNE

COOKING
WITH CULTURE

Please visit our website, www.enslow.com. For a free color catalog of all our high-quality books, call toll free 1-800-398-2504 or fax 1-877-980-4454.

Library of Congress Cataloging-in-Publication Data
Names: Washburne, Sophie, author.
Title: Mexican cuisine / Sophie Washburne.
Description: Buffalo, New York : Enslow Publishing, [2025] | Series:
   Cooking with culture | Includes index.
Identifiers: LCCN 2024002923 | ISBN 9781978540453 (library binding) | ISBN
   9781978540446 (paperback) | ISBN 9781978540460 (ebook)
Subjects: LCSH: Cooking, Mexican–Juvenile literature. |
   Food–Mexico–History–Juvenile literature. | LCGFT: Cookbooks.
Classification: LCC TX716.M4 W38 2025 | DDC 641.5972–dc23/eng/20240212
LC record available at https://lccn.loc.gov/2024002923

Published in 2025 by
Enslow Publishing
2544 Clinton Street
Buffalo, NY 14224

Portions of this work were originally authored by Kevin Pearce and published as *Foods of Mexico*. All new material in this edition authored by Sophie Washburne.

Designer: Leslie Taylor
Editor: Caitie McAneney

Photo credits: Cover (photo) lunamarina/Shutterstock.com; Series Art (background icon pattern) porcelaniq/Shutterstock.com; Series Art (series logo) lukeruk/Shutterstock.com; p. 5 LuLuraschi/Shutterstock.com, (inset) Foodio/Shutterstock.com; p. 7 karamysh/Shutterstock.com; p. 9 Brent Hofacker/Shutterstock.com; p. 11 (pozole) hlphoto/Shutterstock.com, (elote) Konstantin Kopachinsky/Shutterstock.com; p. 13 OScar HMz/Shutterstock.com; p. 15 Elena Veselova/Shutterstock.com; p. 17 Jacopo ventura/Shutterstock.com; p. 19 Yulia Furman/Shutterstock.com; p. 21 david olivera/Shutterstock.com.

Printed in the United States of America

CPSIA compliance information: Batch #CSENS25: For further information contact Enslow Publishing at 1-800-398-2504.

Find us on

Contents

Exploring Mexico 4

Important Ingredients 6

Native Foods 8

Recipe: Guacamole 9

Cooking with Corn 10

Mexican Specialties 12

Meat and Fish 14

Unique Dishes 16

Delicious Drinks 18

Tasty Treats 20

Glossary 22

For More Information 23

Index 24

Words in the glossary appear in **bold** type the first time they are used in the text.

Exploring Mexico

Mexican food is a big part of life both in its home country and its neighbor, the United States. That's because Mexico and the United States share a border. That means they also share their **culture** and foods.

FOOD FOR THOUGHT

SOME FOODS YOU MAY THINK ARE MEXICAN ARE ACTUALLY "TEX-MEX," OR A MIX OF TEXAN AND MEXICAN CUISINES. ONE EXAMPLE IS NACHOS.

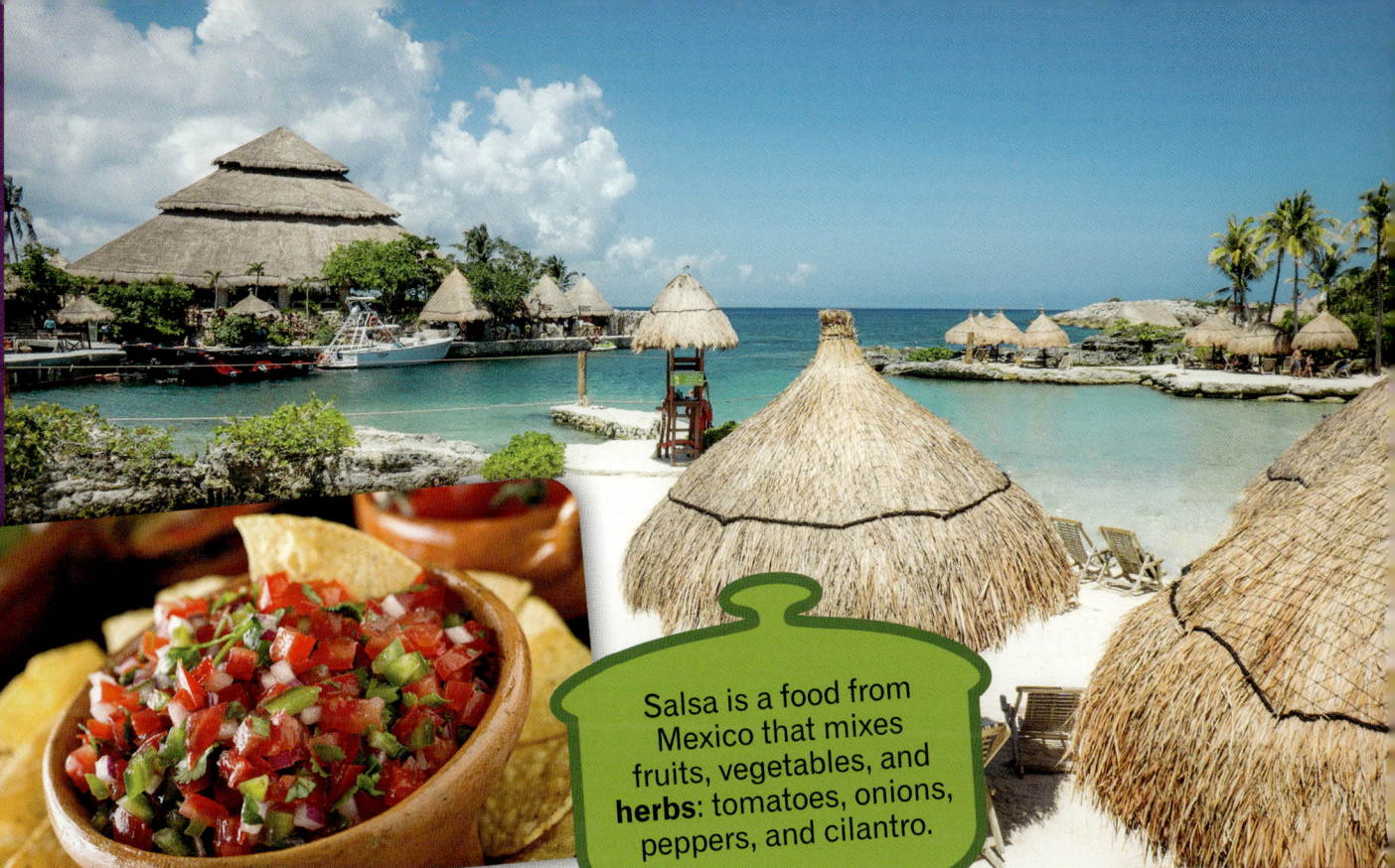

Salsa is a food from Mexico that mixes fruits, vegetables, and **herbs**: tomatoes, onions, peppers, and cilantro.

Mexico has a **diverse** landscape with forests and deserts, as well as rivers and beaches. For thousands of years, native Mexicans learned to farm in all of these landscapes. The mix of foods makes up the Mexican **cuisine** we enjoy today.

Important Ingredients

Traditional crops are still important to Mexican cuisine. The three most important foods are corn, squash, and beans. These crops were grown by Native peoples in Mexico before the Spanish arrived in 1517.

FOOD FOR THOUGHT

BEANS ARE CALLED *FRIJOLES* IN MEXICO. THEY ARE USED IN MANY DISHES, INCLUDING REFRIED BEANS AND *ENFRIJOLADAS* (TORTILLAS AND BEAN SAUCE).

Tortillas are cooked on a hot grill or stove.

Corn is the main **ingredient** in the flat, round bread called a tortilla. Sometimes, tortillas are eaten alongside a main dish. Other times, they're filled with food, folded or rolled, and eaten as the main dish. While some people eat flour tortillas, corn tortillas are more common in Mexico.

Native Foods

Mexican people use other native crops in their meals too. These include tomatoes, peppers, and sweet potatoes. Avocados are used in a dish called guacamole. Mexicans use a stone tool called a *molcajete* to crush ingredients together.

The Yucatán **peninsula** is in southeast Mexico. The Maya who lived there shaped the cuisine, which includes hard-boiled eggs and turkey. Another Mayan food is chocolate. It was made as a hot drink that included chili peppers.

Guacamole

Ingredients

2 ripe avocados
1 chopped jalapeño
1/4 onion, chopped
1 chopped tomato
1/4 cup cilantro
1 teaspoon lime juice
salt (to taste)

Equipment

knife
bowl
spoon or fork for mashing

Steps

1. Peel the avocado. Take out the pit.
2. Mash the avocado in a bowl.
3. Add the jalapeño, onion, tomato, and cilantro.
4. Add in lime juice and salt, tasting as you go.

FOOD FOR THOUGHT

FRUITS SUCH AS **PLANTAINS**, PAPAYAS, AND TOMATILLOS ARE ALSO FOUND THROUGHOUT MEXICO.

Cooking with Corn

Elote is a grilled corn cob covered in spices. It's common to find elote at **street vendors** in Mexico.

Tacos, burritos, and quesadillas have become a popular part of U.S. cuisine. In all of these, corn tortillas are filled with foods such as meat, beans, vegetables, and cheese.

pozole

Corn is boiled to make pozole, a thick stew.

elote

Enchiladas are another popular dish. These are tortillas dipped in chili sauce. It's easy to find a dish with corn tortillas in Mexico!

FOOD FOR THOUGHT

CORN IS IMPORTANT FOR TAMALES TOO. IN THIS DISH, THICK CORNMEAL PASTE COVERS A FILLING OF MEAT AND PEPPERS. THEN THE TAMALES ARE WRAPPED IN CORNHUSKS AND STEAMED.

Mexican Specialties

Imagine you go to a Mexican restaurant, but you don't speak Spanish—the main language of Mexico. Here are some Spanish words for Mexican specialties: *carne* (meat), *pescado* (fish), and *postre* (dessert).

FOOD FOR THOUGHT

SOPA DE LIMA IS CHICKEN SOUP WITH LIME JUICE. THE SPANISH WORD FOR "SOUP" IS SOPA, AND THE WORD FOR "LIME" IS LIMA.

Poblano peppers are very spicy! Chile relleno is a Mexican dish with a stuffed poblano pepper.

Beans are served with many dishes. Pinto beans are often used in northern Mexico, while black beans are popular in southern Mexico. *Mole poblano* is a sauce made from chocolate and peppers. It's spicy and it's often served over chicken.

Meat and Fish

Some foods arrived with the Spanish in the 1500s. Spain ruled Mexico for 300 years. The Spanish culture greatly affected Mexican cuisine. The Spanish brought livestock, including cattle, pigs, and chickens, to add to the cuisine. Today, grilled beef is called carne asada in Mexico.

FOOD FOR THOUGHT

THE BAJA CALIFORNIA PENINSULA IN NORTHWEST MEXICO IS WHERE FISH TACOS BECAME FAMOUS. THERE ARE PLENTY OF FISH HERE IN BOTH THE PACIFIC OCEAN AND GULF OF CALIFORNIA.

Northern Mexico was the birthplace of *barbacoa*, a method of steaming meat over coals in a pit. The word "barbecue" comes from this cooking style. In southern Mexico, chicken is more common than beef.

Unique Dishes

Mexico has many foods that are **unique**—and even unusual to people outside of the culture. In southern Mexico, grasshoppers are fried, spiced, and eaten as snacks. The meat of lizards called iguanas is eaten there as well.

In desert areas, prickly pear cactuses are used for food. Called *nopal*, these prickly pears must have their thorns removed before eating.

FOOD FOR THOUGHT

IN CENTRAL MEXICO, THE EGGS OF BLACK ANTS ARE BOILED AND EATEN IN TORTILLAS.

In coastal areas, people enjoy foods such as squid and octopus.

They're said to have lots of **nutrients** and were used by the Aztecs long ago as medicine.

17

Delicious Drinks

A drink in Mexico is called a *bebida*. Mexicans have many cold, sweet drinks for hot days. *Agua de jamaica* is a deep red or purple drink made from flowers. Fruit juices in Mexico include watermelon and orange juice.

FOOD FOR THOUGHT

A HOT DRINK CALLED ATOLE—A MIX OF CORN OR RICE MEAL, WATER, AND SPICES—IS PREPARED FOR HOLIDAYS, SUCH AS DÍA DE LOS MUERTOS (THE DAY OF THE DEAD).

atole

This atole is served alongside special breads and treats for Día de los Muertos.

Horchata is a refreshing milky drink. It is often made of plant-based ingredients like nut milks or rice. Cinnamon and vanilla make this drink sweet and delicious! Mexican hot chocolate is a hot drink made of cinnamon, chili peppers, and chocolate.

19

Tasty Treats

When a Mexican meal is done, it's time for dessert. People buy sweet breads from bread bakeries, which are called *panaderías*. They buy pastries from pastry shops called *pastelerías*. Sugar skulls and candies are eaten for special holidays like Día de los Muertos.

Flan is a famous Mexican dessert made of eggs, milk, and sugar. Dulce de leche is a heated, sweetened milk that turns into a type of caramel sauce. It's often served over cake for celebrations. There are so many Mexican foods to celebrate!

In many places in Mexico, street vendors sell paletas, or frozen treats, on hot days.

FOOD FOR THOUGHT

PAN DULCE, OR CONCHAS, IS A SWEET BREAD EATEN IN MEXICO FOR BREAKFAST OR WITH OTHER MEALS.

Glossary

cuisine: A style of cooking.

culture: The beliefs and ways of life of a group of people.

diverse: Different or varied.

herb: A low-growing plant used to add a taste to food.

ingredient: A part of a mixture.

nutrient: Something a living thing needs to grow and stay alive.

peninsula: A narrow piece of land that extends into water from the mainland

plantain: A greenish-yellow fruit that looks like a banana.

street vendor: One who sells goods from a cart or stand on a street.

traditional: In a manner following past actions or ways of life.

unique: One of a kind.

For More Information

Books

Hansen, Grace. *Mexico*. Minneapolis, MN: Abdo Kids, 2020.

Silva, Sadie. *Day of the Dead*. Buffalo, NY: Enslow Publishing, 2023.

Websites

Mexico
kids.nationalgeographic.com/geography/countries/article/mexico
Discover exciting facts about Mexico with National Geographic Kids.

Salsa
www.pbs.org/food/recipes/salsa/
Try making your own salsa with this recipe from PBS Kids!

Index

avocado, 8, 9

Aztec, 17

barbacoa, 15

beans, 6, 10, 13

burritos, 10

carnitas, 15

chocolate, 8, 13, 19

cilantro, 5, 9

corn, 6, 7, 10, 11, 18

dulce de leche, 20

enchiladas, 11

flan, 20

guacamole, 8, 9

juice, 18

Maya, 8

nachos, 4

nopal, 16

pan dulce, 21

peppers, 5, 8, 11, 13, 19

quesadillas, 10

salsa, 5

squash, 6

tacos, 10, 14

tamales, 11

Tex-Mex, 4

tortillas, 6, 7, 10, 11, 16

Yucatán peninsula, 8